Stained Glass Projects

FOR THE HOME

STAINED GLASS PROJECTS
FOR THE HOME

BLANDFORD

Contents

Introduction

Louis Comfort Tiffany

Tiffany & Company is a name that even a decade ago would have evoked immediate associations with the world-famous American jewellers. The appearance of the film version of Truman Capote's novel *Breakfast at Tiffany's*, and the newspaper announcements that Richard Burton had bought one of the most expensive diamonds in the world for Elizabeth Taylor at Tiffany's, made the store's name synonymous with luxury jewellery. In the last decade, however, Tiffany lamps and other decorative objects have become so sought after by collectors that they seem to have overtaken Tiffany jewellery in popularity. It must be rare for one family to become famous in two completely different areas.

Louis Comfort Tiffany (1848–1933) was the son of Charles Louis Tiffany, the founder of the New York silversmiths and jewellery firm. He certainly had an easier start in life than many of his artist contemporaries as he was financially independent; not everyone who is interested in glass manufacture also has the means to carry out his ideas by building his own glass-making factory and his own glasshouse! Nevertheless, Tiffany's success cannot be explained by wealth alone. In addition to his talent as a painter, he also demonstrated a larger than average share of curiosity and a willingness to experiment.

In the 1880s Tiffany began to turn towards craftsmanship as a career. In those days art was not regarded as being automatically accessible to everyone. The idea of manufacturing beautiful everyday objects and of combining artistic beauty with the needs of everyday life in this way had already been mooted by William Morris (1834–96). Louis Comfort Tiffany had met Morris and may even have been influenced by him. However, while Morris never managed to bridge the gap between manufacturing functional items for the homes of the rich upper middle class and manufacturing those objects at reasonable prices, this goal was Tiffany's right from the start. Long before the artists of the Bauhaus were designing beautiful and functional furniture, lamps and everyday objects for mass production between 1919 and 1933, Tiffany both recognized the need and opportunities for craftsmanship in the industrial age and exploited them. His wish to make beautiful everyday objects accessible to the general public, his artistic productivity and, above all, his business sense enabled him to influence substantially the evolution of skilled craftsmanship.

His interest in designing and producing glass objects was aroused on a trip to Europe during which he had visited the cathedral at Chartres in France, when he had been deeply impressed by the intensity and jewel-like brilliance of the stained glass windows. He discovered that the techniques for manufacturing this kind of glass seemed to have been lost, as the glass available in the 1880s was not nearly as brilliant as the glass he had seen at Chartres. At the end of the nineteenth century the usual technique of manufacturing coloured glass was to paint ground glass with a brush on to a sheet of glass and then to melt it into the surface. Tiffany began his own experiments, founding the Tiffany Glass Company in 1885. While the first of his stained glass pictures were being admired at exhibitions, he was building two factories to produce glass objects, both of which, unfortunately, were destroyed by fire. In 1893 he acquired another factory, and in the following years made glass of a beauty that has not been equalled.

In quick succession he founded several companies in which he worked with other artists to design beautiful yet useful objects. The Tiffany Studios were founded in 1902 to design and produce fabrics, carpets, furniture, mosaics, leaded glass windows, vases, everyday objects, mirrors and even entire interiors of houses. Louis Comfort Tiffany personally supervised the organization of the Studios and the designs emanating from them, and from 1894 onwards he was also a director in the family firm, becoming artistic director on his father's death in 1902. He left behind a huge body of artwork, and his oil paintings, watercolours, tempera paintings, glass items and book designs are intimately bound up with both the Impressionist and Art Nouveau movements.

Instead of putting lead around individual pieces of glass Tiffany invented the technique of wrapping copperfoil around the edges and soldering it, thereby enriching this whole area of artistic activity with a practice that has been both fruitful and long lasting. Some motifs can only be made by this method, while others are manufactured more delicately and more easily. This will be described in detail in Chapter 2, Techniques.

A final word of caution. Louis Comfort Tiffany was not only the inventor of a certain type of glass, but, as an artist, he was also the designer and creator of a number of glass objects. Therefore the name 'Tiffany glass' can be confusing and the description 'original Tiffany glass' does not necessarily mean you have acquired glass fashioned by Louis Comfort Tiffany himself, but only that this is an object manufactured according to his techniques.

An original Tiffany window.

Glass — A Brief History

Assyrian cuneiform texts dating from the period c.1700 to 700 BC indicate that glass has been known to man for thousands of years. Over the years the techniques for manufacturing and processing glass have been constantly improved and developed so that more and more uses for the material have been found. Today, we could not imagine life without glass. It is used in the manufacture of dozens of everyday objects, in art and in craft as well as in science and technology. Nowadays, faced as we are with an enormous range of glass products, many of which are destined to be thrown away, it is easy to forget that in the sixteenth and seventeenth centuries glass was regarded as a luxury item.

The oldest surviving recipe for the manufacture of glass originated from the library of the Assyrian king, Ashurbanipal, who reigned c.700 BC. Surprisingly, the Romans used little glass, most of their utensils being made of ceramic. Only in the Middle Ages did glass begin to be used more widely. Small pieces of glass or mirror were, according to the prevailing fashion, worn on belts or around the neck c.1100, which indicates that glass was still considered to be a precious commodity. The first great age of glass art began in the thirteenth century, and it was at this time that the stained glass windows of the cathedral at Chartres were made.

In the fourteenth and fifteenth centuries glass windows came to be used in the houses of the wealthier middle classes. In Venice the glass factory on the island of Murano succeeded in producing colourless glass c.1500, and the factory acquired a reputation for the production of glass and glass vessels at the time of the Renaissance that it has retained to this day.

In the sixteenth century demand for glass increased sharply. Until this time glass had been appreciated mostly for its intrinsic beauty, but now, as interest in the natural sciences began to grow, it came to be valued for utilitarian purposes, and it was used in the manufacture of

A hand-blown glass vase in the Roman style.

A basket made of blown antique glass.

travelling hour-glasses and for such optical items as spectacles, microscopes and telescopes. In 1688 a technique was developed for making molten glass into plate glass and mirror glass, and thereafter large sheets of glass could be manufactured without difficulty. This gave the glass industry a further boost.

The many innovations and inventions that occurred in the fields of physics and chemistry in the Age of Enlightenment in the eighteenth century cannot be discussed here, but two dates are worth noting to illustrate how, throughout history, new ways of using glass have been found and to show that it is more than likely that we have not, even now, exhausted all the potential uses of this substance. In 1846 Carl Zeiss founded a famous workshop in Jena in Germany to produce optical instruments of hitherto unimagined precision and, later, fire-proof glassware for cooking. Now, more than a hundred years later, with the emergence of fibre-optic technology, the factory is working on a completely new quality of glass, the full importance and effects of which cannot yet be appreciated.

A cylindrical vase made of antique glass that was blown by mouth and finished by traditional glass-blowing methods.

Lumps of coloured glass from a glass factory.

Glass — The Material

In its primitive state glass is basically molten sand. Ordinary glass contains 65–75 per cent silicic acid (quartz sand, silicon dioxide), 10–20 per cent of an alkaline flux and 10–20 per cent calcium. The actual glass-forming substance is the silicic acid; the soda or potash is added as an alkaline flux to lower the melting temperature; and the calcium ensures the mechanical and chemical stability of the substance.

Coloured glass is produced by adding metal oxides to the molten mixture. The oxides cause the glass to allow light of only certain wavelengths to pass through it, and they, in effect, produce the individual colours. Paradoxically, therefore, coloured glass is not really coloured — that is, it contains no colour pigments. The different colour effects are obtained by mixing in a wide variety of substances. Louis Comfort Tiffany, for example, used saltpetre, bone-meal ash, sodium chloride (cooking salt), manganese, cobalt, copper oxide, arsenic and probably a few more that he did not divulge.

The Tiffany techniques allow a whole range of types of glass to be manufactured, and these are offered for sale by the Tiffany Studios and are available in many craft shops.

Lampshades are mainly made of *opalescent glass*, which is slightly marbled. The transparency of opalescent glass ranges from the completely opaque to the wholly transparent. If the glass is opaque, only very little light passes through it when it is held in front of a light source. If it is transparent, light can pass through almost unhindered. All types of opalescent glass allow light to be distributed evenly over its surface, so that it seems as though the glass itself, not the lamp, is glowing, and it creates a gentle, soft light. It is usually about 3mm (⅛in) thick.

Cathedral glass and *coloured glass* are especially suitable for windows because they are very transparent, but they can also be used for highlights within a lampshade. Because these types of glass are manufactured almost exclusively by machine, they are inexpensive and are, therefore, especially suitable for a beginner's first attempts at working with glass.

Types of glass that have a rough or textured back are often known as *ripple glass*. This kind of glass is particularly suitable for floral motifs.

Flower petals and leaves made of ripple glass have an appearance of depth because of the texturing. However, ripple glass is hard to work with as its textured back does not always allow it to be snapped exactly along the scored lines.

Antique glass is blown by mouth and is transparent. Its colours are clear and brilliant, and it varies in thickness between 1.5mm and 4.5mm (1/16–1/4in).

There is a distinction between *hand-rolled* and *machine-rolled* types of glass. Hand-rolled glass is generally more difficult to score as its surface is never quite even. However, these irregularities give additional charm to items made from it. The blending of shades of light and dark colours looks more natural and harmonious, while machine-made glass often has shades that vary abruptly and look harsh together. Machine-made glass, however, has the advantages of being easier to work with and of being cheaper.

When you come to work with glass you will probably notice that some colours are more difficult to score than others. For example, glass in the colour range of white to green is much easier to score than glass made with selenium in the colour ranges of yellow, red and orange. However, in

Cathedral glass is characterized by high transparency. It is extremely suitable for making windows.

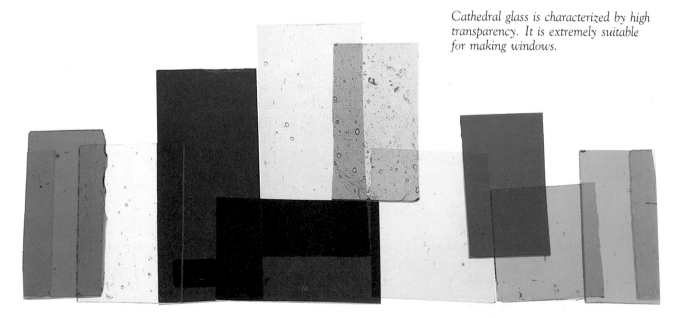

Opalescent glass is available in different colours and textures.

time you will acquire a feel for the amount of pressure you need to exert when scoring various types and colours of glass.

Opalescent glass is not cheap, so before you begin, plan carefully how you will arrange the individual shapes on the sheet of glass you have bought. By giving some thought to the placing of the templates you should be able to obtain a large number of pieces from one sheet. However, as a beginner, you should reckon to lose about 30 per cent through breakage. For this reason, you should always buy a little more glass than you will actually need. Generally, I would recommend a few

trial runs using simple, inexpensive window glass. (The techniques of cutting and snapping glass are discussed in Chapter 2.)

Opalescent glass allows light to be evenly distributed over the entire surface. It is especially suitable for making lampshades.

Uroboros glass is manufactured in the United States. Extremely fine flakes of glass are laid on a ready-made sheet of glass and then melted into the substrate at about 600°C (1112°F).

Glass 'jewels' and 'diamonds' come in a wide range of shapes and sizes. The 'jewels' are especially useful for incorporating into lamps because they suit Art Nouveau designs perfectly and also create charming highlights. Glass 'diamonds' are cut with facets and can bend light in many ways. They are an excellent way of introducing an extra dimension into the frame of a mirror, for example. Glass nuggets are irregularly shaped, small stones, which are best suited to mosaic work.

Kokomo glass is another type of glass manufactured in the United States. It is characterized by the myriad of colours it contains.

The density of Chicago glass varies from transparent to opaque.

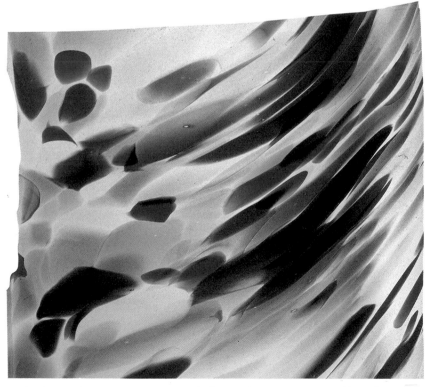

The charm of antique glass lies in its brilliant colours. Because it is blown by mouth, it usually contains several air bubbles, which are sometimes lens shaped and sometimes shaped like tiny channels, and these can bend light in interesting ways.

Colour and Shape

The choice of suitable glass and especially the combination of different types of glass, requires some taste and an experienced sense of colour. This cannot be stressed enough at this point. However, it is possible to give some general guidance on judging colours and a few tips about the harmonious arrangement of colour and shape.

Each colour has three components. The first is the actual *colour* itself, which is known by the usual names — green, red, pink and so on. The second element of colour is its *intensity*; the same colour may be light or dark, matt or brilliant. The third element is its *value*, which is determined by how close the colour is to black or white. Yellow, for example, is a light colour as it is closer to white and therefore has a higher colour value. A dark colour, such as violet, is closer to black and has a correspondingly lower colour value.

Yellow, red and blue are the three *primary colours*; when added together they create white light and are, therefore, also known as the additive primaries. Orange, violet and green are the so-called *secondary colours*, because they are created from primary colours by direct mixing. All other colours are combinations of these colours.

Colour harmony can be achieved only by carefully balancing the colour itself, and its intensity and value. The size and colour of the object in question are, of course, other aspects to be taken into consideration. A shade that dominates others in terms of colour, intensity and value should ideally not be used for large areas. Compared with pictures, prints and posters, which reflect light, glass objects allow light to pass through them, and this means that the individual colours are not clearly separated but appear to the viewer to blend together and to overlap. Neighbouring colours will always influence each other. There are, too, additional factors that determine the

character of the colour of glass: the *structure* of the glass, its *thickness* and its *transparency*. A less dominant colour can, for example, be upgraded in value by using thick or textured glass, while a dominant colour can be toned down by using very transparent glass.

If you do not feel very sure about your colour sense, you should perhaps begin with compositions in shades of one colour and highlight them sparingly here and there with a more conspicuous colour. It is a good idea to be guided by the principle of complementary colours. In the colour circle on the opposite page, the complementary colours are those placed opposite each other: red and green, blue and orange, and yellow and violet. Shades of blue and brown are very suitable for the background of a glass picture or for the frame or edge of an object. Red and orange should be used with restraint, although their effect can be softened by using white glass nearby. Yellow is a very aggressive colour and brilliant shades of yellow should be avoided. Soft shades of yellow, however, combine well with blue. Green is the one colour that is compatible with most other colours. Colours with a touch of grey in them are useful for toning down and softening strong colours.

Before you begin to make your glass object, I would suggest that you lay the coloured glass of your choice on a window sill and look at it in daylight. If you are planning to make a lampshade, hold the glass in front of an artificial light source, as the glass will appear to change colour according to the ambient light.

Your selection of colours should be decided in conjunction with the shape of the object you are intending to make. Even the shape itself should be considered carefully in terms of harmony and balance. Although it may seem that the world is being constantly enriched with new shapes and forms, generally, most 'new' forms can be reduced to a common origin, and the seeming variety around us is in no way as great as we might at first sight believe.

Throughout the development of shape and form, which itself may be studied as an aspect of the history of art, basic and classical shapes and forms have evolved. Some of these shapes have their origins in nature, some in art. Many geometric shapes are known to be abstract forms of shapes that are known in nature — for example, a leaf and a triangle — and although the shapes can be infinitely varied, it is impossible to deny their origins. Even if you wish to create something completely new, you will inevitably be influenced by historic shapes and forms. Nature, art and geometry are the teachers from which all can be learned.

Opposite: different shades of the same colours; on the left, warm shades of red, and, on the right, cool shades of blue. Designs that use various shades of the same colour can never go wrong.

According to Johannes Itten, this colour circle demonstrates what van Gogh wrote about the 'great truths about colour'. Itten wrote: 'In nature there are three elementary colours that cannot be reduced down to other colours, and these are the primary colours, yellow red and blue. When any two of these are mixed, the secondary colours, orange, green and violet are created. Any secondary colour mixed from two primary colours will provide a contrast to the other primary colour, and together these colours will appear in greatest intensity; they are called complementary colours.' Complementary colours are also called contrasting colours, and if the artist or photographer has not already added them, the human eye so desires to see them that it even creates them itself.

Colour circle by Johnannes Itten,
Kunst der Farbe (The Art of Colour),
Otto Maier Verlag, Ravensburg.)

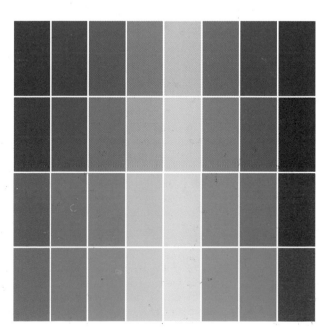

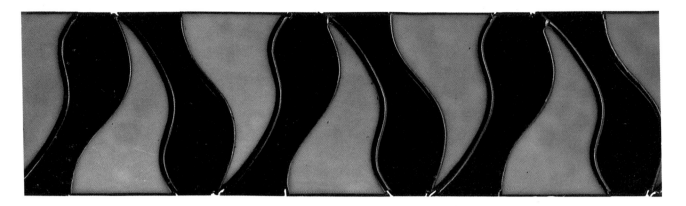

Some of the major movements in art — Art Nouveau, Art Deco, Secessionism and even Pop-art, for example — are especially rich in inspiration for the Tiffany artist. More than at any other period in the history of art and design, the early years of this century saw artists making mirrors, lamps and other functional items, and visiting an exhibition of objects from this period will suggest some excellent ideas for projects of your own.

In addition to copying classical shapes, you can, of course, give your own feelings for form and design free rein. In general, design is the discipline of dividing up a space into shapes, areas and colours, while the development of form is the process of creating a space out of shapes, areas and colours. It is easy to recognize or describe the principles of design or the creation of form when you are using geometric shapes, and if you wish to design a harmonious geometric shape, bear in mind the following compositional precepts.

1 *Repetition* — some elements and shapes will be employed in more than one part of the design.

2 *Rhythm* — the relationship of the elements to each other will follow a certain rhythm or principle; similar elements will not be distributed across the design in a random or in an uneven way but rather in a rhythmic or in a consciously arrhythmic fashion.

3 *Balance* — each individual element derives its effect from its interaction with other, similar elements (rhythm) and from its association with the elements surrounding it. Immediate proximity to one element can emphasize an element or neutralize it, cancel it out or enhance it.

4 *Proportion* — the relationship of the shape of the object to its size and the relationship of the size of individual shapes to each other will determine the overall proportion of the final object.

5 *Vanishing point or focal point* — it is possible that there is a central point, or a central element, to which the other elements appear to be directed. The position of this point within the object is very important, and can be determined only in respect to the angle from which the object is viewed.

There are many possible sources of ideas for geometric shapes. A vast area for research would be Arabic or oriental ornamentation, for example, which have been somewhat neglected by Tiffany artists. If you want to get away from Art Nouveau and Art Deco patterns, you will find ornaments in oriental design that would be extraordinarily well suited to execution in glass. But this is just a suggestion for future projects using Tiffany techniques — a beginner would probably find oriental motifs too difficult to execute.

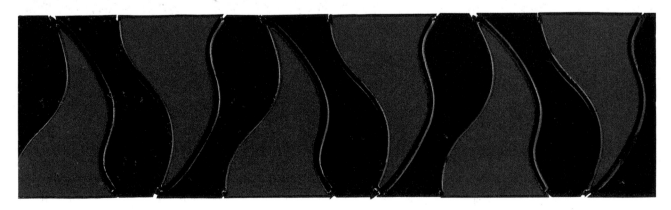

Inside a glass studio. Ideally glass should be transported and stored in an upright position. A professionally equipped workbench of the kind depicted here is not, of course, necessary for anyone who works with glass for a hobby.

1. Tools and Accessories

Before describing the techniques involved, I will first give an overall view of all the tools and materials you will need. I am purposely also mentioning those articles that can normally be found in any house, but it is extremely annoying and disrupting to one's concentration to find, in the middle of working, that one item or another needs to be bought. I have given short descriptions of the special tools that you will use, and you will soon become familiar with their purposes from the explanations of the various working processes. I have, however, avoided recommending specific products. Supplies and prices vary so widely from area to area that it is probably better if everyone finds out for themselves the tools and accessories that are available locally, that they find best for working and that are the least expensive.

Design

To prepare your own design you will need:

☆ Card or cardboard (large enough for the size of the planned object)
☆ Tracing-paper
☆ A felt-tip pen
☆ A soft pencil
☆ A ruler
☆ Adhesive tape and double-sided tape
☆ Ordinary scissors
☆ Template scissors (These not only cut the cardboard but cut away an additional narrow strip of cardboard, which takes into account later soldering seams.)

Cutting

To cut glass you will need:

☆ A firm base made of a laminated fibre or felt
☆ A wax or chinagraph pencil
☆ Sewing-machine oil and petrol (in a 50:50 mix)
☆ A rubber-backed metal ruler

☆ Glass cutters (The best kind are hard metal cutters with only one wheel, which can be followed more easily with the eye when cutting and on which the wheel can be exchanged at the axle when it is worn out; a specially shaped handle makes working much easier, especially for the beginner. After use make sure you brush the little wheel off so that it will turn freely the next time you use it. Clean your glass cutters from time to time with a rag dipped in oil, and oil the axle regularly with a mixture of sewing-machine oil and petrol.)
☆ A small paintbrush
☆ And finally, of course – glass.

Snapping

To break or snap glass you will need:

☆ A grozer or a pair of grozing pliers (These pliers are for removing or grozing small, irregular bits of glass along the edges of a cut.)

18

- ☆ Plate pliers (These are for cutting off narrow strips of glass, which cannot be done by hand.)
- ☆ Running or continental pliers for long cuts (Over a certain length it is not possible to hold the strip to be broken off at the correct angle to the direction of the cut as the pressure exerted by one's hands cannot be distributed evenly along the entire length of the cut. These pliers can be applied to the strip of glass to be broken off along the direction of the cut and pressed together briefly; even if the strip does not break off immediately, you can easily snap it off by hand.)
- ☆ Safety glasses or goggles.

and does not give nearly as neat a finish as machine grinding. Even with a grinding attachment on your drill you will not get far, as you cannot wet grind. Dry grinding is dangerous because tiny glass particles may get into your eyes and lungs. The edges of pieces of glass should be ground so that the copperfoil is not damaged while it is being used to surround the edges of each piece of glass. When you are wet grinding the liquid can spray out; you should, therefore, cover up any furniture in the vicinity with a plastic sheet.)

- ☆ Plastic sheeting
- ☆ Safety glasses or goggles
- ☆ An apron.

Soldering

To solder you will need:

- ☆ Stearin oil or soldering fluid
- ☆ A paintbrush
- ☆ A soldering iron with a stand (minimum 75 watt)
- ☆ Tallow flux
- ☆ Lead–tin solder (50 per cent tin: 50 per cent lead).

Patinating

To patinate you will need:

- ☆ Patina
- ☆ Rubber gloves
- ☆ A cloth or sponge.

Grinding

To grind glass you will need:

- ☆ A soft cotton rag or disposable paper tissue
- ☆ A Styrofoam sheet (the size of the planned object)
- ☆ Pins with plastic heads
- ☆ A grinding machine (Although it is not absolutely necessary to purchase this right at the beginning, it is recommended nevertheless, as grinding by hand is tedious and time consuming

Copperfoiling

For copperfoiling you will need:

- ☆ A knife
- ☆ A small roller
- ☆ Copperfoil (You will need various widths and thicknesses to suit the thickness of the glass; your retailer will advise you when you buy glass, so that you use the correct kind.)
- ☆ Acrylic varnish for mirrors (preferably in a spray can).

Do not be put off by this long list of items that you will need. As making Tiffany-style projects has become increasingly popular and more widespread, the tools have become less expensive. Once you have bought them, your only further expenditure will be on glass. Compared to the value of the objects, which would be very expensive to buy, Tiffany work is a very inexpensive hobby.

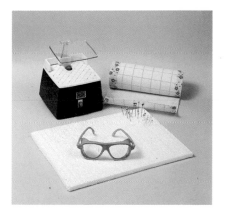

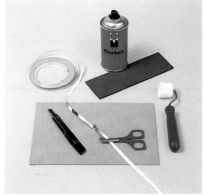

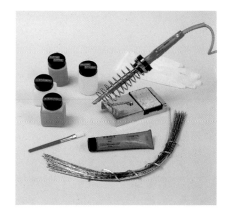

2. Techniques

Design

Design is the foundation of every crafted object or work of art; only geniuses can dispense with it! A professional, too, may have acquired the ability to create a design in his head after a lot of experience, but for a beginner there is one simple rule: spontaneity is no good.

Sometimes things may not move fast enough, so you decide to charge ahead, but generally in such cases the results are disappointing. Not only will you probably make the very obvious mistakes of a first piece of work, but a lot of enthusiasm for your hobby will have gone out of the window. It is much better to spend some time on the design and then to take more pleasure in your first work of art.

You can make designs or templates for Tiffany glass objects yourself or you can buy them. Even a beginner can start with his or her own designs if the object is to be a two-dimensional one with large areas of a single colour. It is very often a beginner's designs for Tiffany mirrors that reveal a surprisingly expressive approach. Things become more difficult with three-dimensional objects such as lampshades, lights and bowls. You should definitely work with bought templates for these projects to begin with, but as you gain confidence you will be able to choose whether you prefer to work with your own ideas or to copy classic Tiffany designs.

Ready-made templates

It is possible to buy kits that contain the outlines of all the pieces you will need. First, you have to transfer the outlines of the templates to tracing-paper. Use a soft pencil so that the paper is not damaged. Then transfer the outlines to a sheet of cardboard. Not until you have done this should you carefully cut out the individual pieces. Use the template scissors, which not only cut the cardboard but also take away a very thin strip that takes into account later soldering seams. Lay the cardboard templates on the appropriate pieces of glass and draw around the edges with a felt-tip pen. Then follow this felt-tip line with a glass cutter. Remember to number the individual pieces of the object both on the cardboard and on the tracing-paper. This will make it easier to assemble them later on.

Transfer your design to a sheet of cardboard.

Copy the sketch on to tracing-paper.

Cut out the individual pieces of cardboard with template scissors.

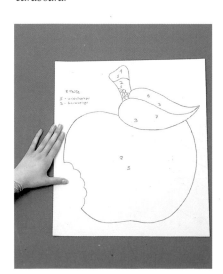

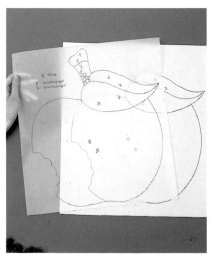

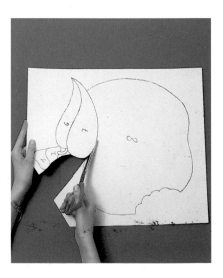

Do not cut up the piece of tracing-paper with the design on it. You should stick it on to a large Styrofoam sheet with a little adhesive tape so that it can be used to position the pieces of glass when they have been ground. Hold the pieces of glass in their correct positions with pins, inserting the pins vertically, not at an angle, through the tracing-paper and into the Styrofoam sheet close to the edge of the glass so that it cannot slip. In this way you will be able to check the arrangement of the colours before the pieces of glass are fixed together, and, if necessary, make any adjustments. In this way, too, the original design is not destroyed, and you could use it again.

It is also possible to buy three-dimensional shapes (or moulds) of Styrofoam segments for objects such as lampshades (see pages 36–8).

The finished mirror, for which bronze and crystal mirror glass were used.

Check the cardboard templates by laying them on the tracing-paper design.

Lay a cardboard template on the selected piece of glass and draw around it with a wax or chinagraph pencil.

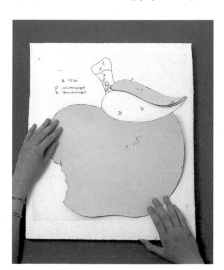

Home-made templates

If you decide to make your own templates, you should draw your design on cardboard and then transfer it to tracing-paper. Number the cardboard templates, and only then should you cut them out. As described above, you should stick the tracing-paper to a Styrofoam sheet. It is also a good idea to colour the individual areas with crayons to give you a first impression of your choice of colours. Avoid very curved edges in your first designs.

If you would like to copy the apple that has been used to illustrate the step-by-step procedure you will find a scale drawing in the chapter on design sketches (see page 77). How to redraw this outline to the desired size is described in Chapter 5. If you do choose to do this, you will be able to follow all the different steps explained here with a real object.

Cutting

Cutting glass requires a lot of practice. To begin with buy a few pieces of broken or waste glass, especially if it is of the same thickness as you will be using later on.

Lay the glass on a smooth, slide-proof surface. I recommend that you use a felt or waxed cloth, which can be stuck or nailed to a firm wooden base.

Holding a glass cutter

Everyone will have to find the best way of holding a glass cutter for themselves. Some people prefer to hold it between their forefinger and thumb (like a pen) or between their forefinger and middle finger. Experiment until you feel comfortable.

You can move the glass cutter away from or towards your body. Generally, however, you only move it towards your body if you want to cut a long line along a ruler (always use a rubber-backed metal ruler). It is easier to watch the scoring of curves in front of a moving hand, and you will be able to exert more control by pushing and pressing the cutter away from your body.

Using a glass cutter

Depending on the thickness and colour of the piece of glass you want to cut, you will have to vary the pressure on the cutter. As already mentioned, some colours — orange and red, for instance — are harder to score and require more pressure.

Note: *to minimize the amount of grinding required later on, you should cut as close as you can to the line you have marked.*

You can hold the glass cutter between your forefinger and middle finger, or

between your forefinger and thumb.

Move the glass cutter along the drawn line or on the inside of it.

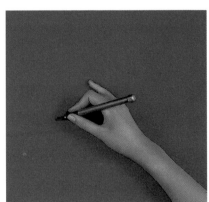

If the line looks whitish after scoring, you have pressed too hard. A correctly executed cut should appear as a fine line on the surface of the glass. Such a line is called a fissure.

Once you have cut a line, you cannot change your mind. On no account should you cut along the same fissure twice, as this would damage the wheel of your cutter. Moreover, the glass along a double fissure either does not snap at all or it breaks badly.

Carry out the scoring operation without stopping and with one smooth movement from beginning to end. Do not take your cutter off the glass, and do not pause or vary the pressure. If it is a long cut, think beforehand where you are going to stand or sit, so that you can carry out the whole action without having to alter the position of your body. Always cut from one edge of the glass to another. However, do not start exactly at the edge, but about 1mm (1/32in) from the edge; you should also stop a fraction before reaching the other edge. In this way you will prevent the cutter slipping over the

edge of the glass and being damaged. This fraction that is not scored will make no difference to the breaking or snapping process later on.

In time you will learn to judge by the sound alone whether glass is going to break cleanly or not. If the glass cutter is used with the correct amount of pressure and with a continuous but vigorous movement, an even, scratching sound is heard. Always try to cut glass on its smooth side.

Care of your glass cutter

Make sure that the wheel of your glass cutter is always well oiled. Do not just lay your glass cutter on the table when you have finished with it, but stand it in a glass or beaker with an oil-soaked cloth at the bottom. Use sewing-machine oil, as recommended in Chapter 1, Tools and Accessories. Even better is a 50:50 mixture of stearin oil and petrol, which does not solidify so quickly.

Auxiliary cuts

When you have to cut along a very curved line, whether it be long or short, extra cuts are always necessary. Even the most experienced people cannot cut sharply re-entrant curves cleanly, and the glass always breaks unevenly.

The first step is to run your glass cutter along the desired line. Do not, however, try to break the glass along this fissure yet. Then carefully work your way towards this line by cutting a series of auxiliary lines nearer and nearer to the main line. Start with a gentle curve and then increase the degree of curvature from one cut to the next until you have almost reached the desired shape. Now you can break off the various curved strips with the grozer.

The deeper the inside curve, the more auxiliary cuts will have to be made. Finally, the remaining piece between the last auxiliary cut and the desired line has to be carefully grozed or worked at with your glass grinder.

Tip: when you are cutting an outside curve, you will find it easier to cut the shape from the sheet of glass if you make several straight (tangential) cuts first.

First, separate the piece of glass you will be working on from the rest of the sheet with several straight cuts.

A few auxiliary cuts will lessen any tension in the glass and make it easier to cut a re-entrant curve.

When you cut a circle begin with tangential cuts.

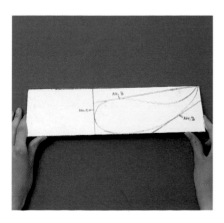

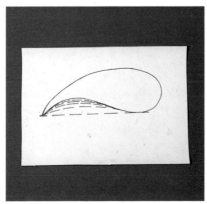

Snapping

You should always wear safety glasses for this operation. They may be a nuisance, but wearing them is definitely safer than doing without. You can also reduce the danger of being hit by splintering pieces of glass by holding the plate of glass you are going to snap at an angle in front of your body, so that the edge furthest away from you is sloping towards the floor. This will help to make sure that any glass splinters will fly away from your body.

By hand

Large pieces of glass can be snapped by hand, and there is, in fact, no other way of dealing with longer, curved lines. However, if the lines are straight and long, you can also use running pliers, especially with thick, metal-oxide-rich glass, and if the glass is rough-backed you should certainly use pliers.

When snapping glass by hand, close your hands into fists, place your forefingers, which should be bent at an angle, under the piece of glass, and place both your thumbs parallel to the cutting line and close to the fissure. You will be able to break the piece of glass, as you would a slab of chocolate, by pressing it with very little effort upwards in the middle and downwards along the edges. You should turn the backs of your hands outwards and downwards to carry out this movement, and remember to make sure that the glass is sloping away from you.

By tapping

Even gently curved lines, which it should be possible to manage without additional straight cuts, are not always easy to snap in one operation. If this happens you should gently tap the reverse side of the scored glass

When you snap glass, always tilt the scored surface away from your face in case any splinters of glass fly out towards you.

Straight cuts can be snapped easily by hand.

When you are cutting thicker glass or cutting curves, it is better to separate the pieces by tapping the glass on the reverse side with the handle of your glass cutter. Longer, more gently curved lines can be snapped by hand.

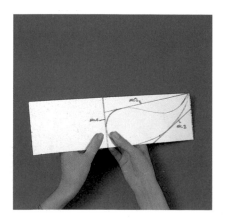

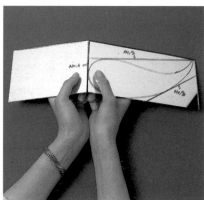

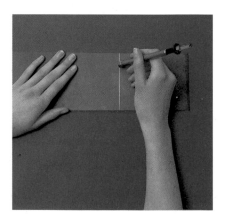

along the fissure with the handle of your glass cutter. Some glass cutters even have a brass knob on the head of the handle, which is especially designed for this purpose.

Always start tapping at the point where the curve is nearest to the edge, and then continue to tap on both sides, gradually working towards the other edge of the piece of glass.

With plate pliers

Although plate pliers are not essential, they are useful for breaking off straight and narrow longer strips of glass.

With running pliers

Only straight lines can be cut with running pliers. The piece you are working on should be at least 4–5cm (1½–2in) wide but no more than a metre (about 1 yard) long. Position the pliers so that they lie in the direction of the fissure and directly over the cut line at the edge of the glass. There should be a little mark or notch on the top of the head of the pliers, and this should align exactly with the cut line. Exert a little pressure on the pliers and at the same time raise the piece of glass slightly. The glass will break cleanly in the desired place.

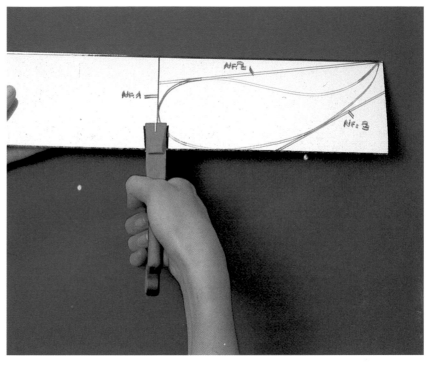

With a grozer

A grozer is the most important pair of pliers you will need to break glass. In theory, all straight and curved lines can be broken with this tool, although in certain situations — as we have seen — other pliers are more suitable. You should always position your grozer at an angle of 90 degrees to the cut line, and the glass is broken with a downwards movement.

Hold your running pliers so that the white mark or notch on the top is turned upwards and position it exactly over the fissure. Move the pliers forwards in the direction of the cutting line until they rest against the edge of the glass plate.

Glass breaking pliers can be used to break off longish pieces of glass.

Grozers are used for breaking off narrower, smaller pieces of glass.

Small edges of glass that are left after snapping can be snipped off with grozers.

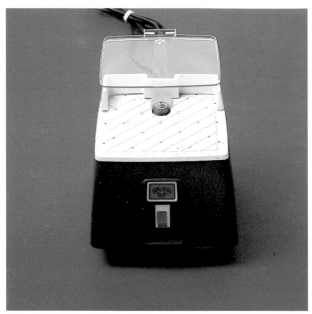

A glass grinding machine will speed up your work considerably.

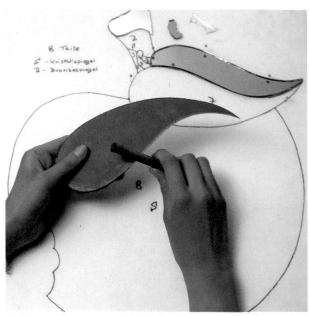

If the initial cut was made with precision, a simple grinding stone (carborundum file) may be all you need.

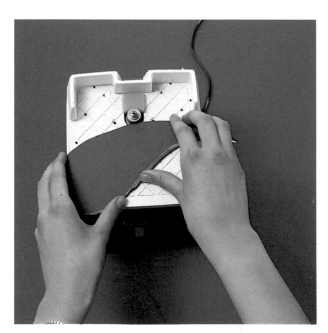

Mirror glass should always be ground with the reverse side facing upwards.

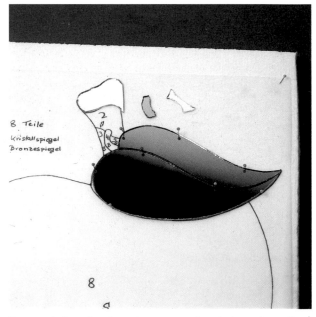

Pieces of glass that have been ground and cleaned are fixed with pins on top of tracing-paper on a Styrofoam base.

Grinding

Snapping glass usually leaves some sharp burrs and irregularities on the edge of the individual pieces, and these must be ground to a smooth edge so that the copperfoil used later around the edges is not damaged and can adhere neatly. In addition, the fissure will not always have run exactly along the wax pencil line you drew originally, and a little more glass will need to be removed so that the shapes fit perfectly together. You should, therefore, grind the edge until the remainder of the wax pencil line has just disappeared. As you work, check by comparing the piece of glass with the original template.

Full instructions for using a glass grinding machine usually come with the machine, and I will not therefore dwell on this aspect in great depth. However, you must remember that the grinding head turns in an anti-clockwise direction. Gently move the glass to be ground along the head and against the cutting direction. Abrupt movements or too much pressure can cause tiny hair-line cracks along the edge. Be especially careful with mirrors. Turn them so that the reverse side is upwards to avoid damaging the reflecting layer. By stopping in one place for just a second you can cut curves into the edge of the glass.

Always wet grind. The grinding fluid is contained in the bottom of the grinding machine, and it is drawn up automatically through the turning motion of the head. It cools the head and binds the glass splinters that are being removed.

Cleaning

After grinding each of the pieces must be cleaned. Assuming that they now correspond exactly to the shapes of the original templates, they can be fixed in the correct positions with pins. To clean the glass you should preferably use a conventional ammonium chloride solution from a spray gun, which can be applied with paper towel. Dry each piece thoroughly, making sure that the edges are completely dry before they are wrapped with copperfoil.

Copperfoiling or the Tiffany Technique

The copperfoil technique is often called the Tiffany technique because it was developed by Louis Comfort Tiffany. It would not be possible to solder the pieces of glass without copperfoil because lead–tin solder goes not adhere to glass. The edges of each individual piece of glass are, therefore, first wrapped in copperfoil, the inside of which is covered with a glass adhesive. Through soldering lead–tin solder and copper combine to create a substance that is stable enough even for large objects. The attractive and sometimes essential combination of copperfoil technique and lead glazing is further discussed on pages 44–8.

Copperfoil can be bought in widths ranging from 3mm to 10mm

(1/8–1/4in) and in different thicknesses. The width and thickness you use will depend partly on the thickness and size of the piece of glass, and partly on the overall size of the planned object. The wider and thicker the foil, the stronger will be the soldered seam. For this reason, large pieces of glass, even if they are thin, will have to be wrapped in correspondingly wider or thicker foil, because the soldered seams will have to support a greater weight. Large, heavy objects — mirrors and lampshades, for example — have to carry a considerable weight, especially at the top, and this weight places a heavy load on the seams. Until you have acquired enough experience, discuss the width and thickness of the foil you will need with an expert retailer or with someone who has considerable experience with the Tiffany technique. In general, objects look more delicate and graceful when narrow copperfoil is used, because the thinner soldered seams are less conspicuous and therefore enhance the glass sections.

Copperfoil is available in rolls that are about 33m (36 yards) long. Although they are not cheap, dispensers in which rolls of foil of different widths and thicknesses can be kept next to each other are extremely useful. It is much quicker to wrap the edges of the glass from a dispenser. Whether you are wrapping by hand or from a dispenser, however, you must first position the foil along the edge of the glass and press it down slightly before cutting it off. Make sure that the foil protrudes evenly on both the right and left sides of the edge. When you have wrapped foil all round the edge of the piece of glass, allow an overlap at the ends of 2–4mm (1/16–1/4in) and stick the overlap over the beginning of the foil. Now press the protruding foil edges on to the surface of the glass with your fingers. Then run a small roller over the foil along all three surfaces — edge, top surface and reverse — to press it down evenly. Make sure there are no air bubbles between the foil and the surfaces of the glass. As lead–tin solder can run only where there is copperfoil, you should make sure that the solder seam is straight and parallel to the edge of the glass by correcting any tiny irregularities with a small sharp knife.

Lay the finished piece on the Styrofoam base.

Acrylic varnish for mirrors

During the soldering process you will be using a fluid that is so strong that it will corrode the laminate on the back of mirrors so that ugly marks appear on the front. For this reason, the back of mirrors must be treated differently. A special varnish can be used that does not allow the soldering fluid to penetrate to, and so damage, the laminate. Either acrylic varnish or shellac is suitable. There is such a vast range of varnishes, all with different chemical components, that it is impossible to make any general recommendations. Try out the various types of varnish for yourself. Paint or spray a small fragment of mirror glass, treat it with soldering fluid and then leave it for a few days. Although time consuming, it is worth conducting the experiment because you will know for certain which types of varnish will save you from unpleasant surprises.

Copperfoil that is 6.5mm (1/4in) wide is suitable for the apple-shaped mirror.

Make sure the copperfoil is smooth and adheres evenly around the piece of glass.

Irregularities or lumps in the copperfoil along sharp curves can be corrected with a small knife.

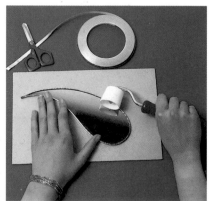

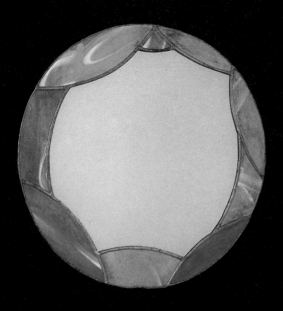

A round mirror with a frame of
iridescent Merry-go-round glass.

A fan-shaped mirror made of crystal,
bronze and gold mirror glass.

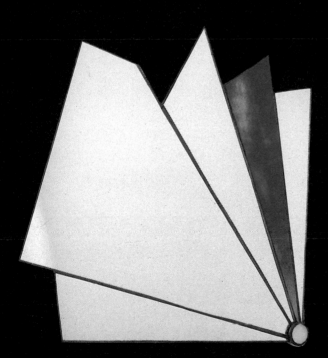

This brooch of mirror glass has a
conspicuous segment of iridescent
Merry-go-round glass.

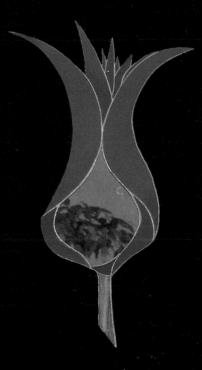

Cutting and copperfoiling the large,
pointed petals of this tulip required
considerable expertise.

Soldering

Before you start soldering you should pin all the individual pieces of glass, in their correct positions, to the sheet of Styrofoam. You must assemble the object, or at least part of it, correctly before you begin because the relative positions of the pieces of glass cannot be altered once they have been soldered.

First, paint the copperfoil with soldering fluid or with stearin oil. The fluid will facilitate the reaction between the wire solder and the copperfoil. Briefly dip the warm soldering iron into a dish of soldering tallow to remove any particles of dirt on the tip of the soldering iron so that the lead–tin solder will flow more easily. You should dip the soldering iron regularly into the soldering tallow while you work.

Then begin spot soldering. The individual pieces of glass should be joined in this way before the seams are completely soldered. Depending on the size of the piece of glass, allow between two and four spots of lead–tin solder to drop on to the edges of

the corners. You can either hold the wire solder against the desired spot and touch it briefly with the soldering iron, or you can let the drop slide off the tip of the soldering iron.

When you have finished spot soldering, you can remove the pins from the Styrofoam sheet and lay your work on a wooden surface. If any pieces do not appear to fit

perfectly in their proper positions, you can apply more solder by melting the soldered spot again briefly with your soldering iron.

If the pieces of glass fit together well you can start soldering the seams; this process is called rough soldering. Turn your work over, because the back should be soldered before the front; if you are making a three-dimensional object, the inside

Note: *do not spend too long soldering a piece of glass because the heat could cause it to break. The laminate on the reverse of a mirror is also susceptible to heat damage. When you are soldering the back of a mirror, proceed very carefully and stop from time to time.*

Before soldering, all the pieces of glass should be foiled and pinned to tracing-paper.

When you are spot soldering, the individual pieces are connected with lead-tin solder at several points.

During rough soldering, apply generous amounts of lead-tin solder to the seams.

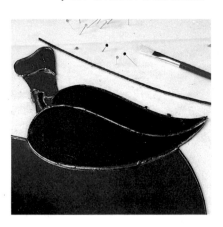

should be soldered before the outside. Pass the wire solder and the soldering iron simultaneously over the copperfoil, making sure that any gaps are well filled. It does not matter if the lead–tin falls through the gaps and congeals in lumps on the other side. These irregularities can be removed later. Then turn your work over and rough solder the other side.

Before you start fine soldering, you should clean your work again. Then carefully paint all the seams with soldering fluid before passing your soldering iron along the seams once more. Move the soldering iron smoothly and without stopping in the middle of a seam — if possible, do not stop along the whole length of a simple piece of glass. If you want to create especially even, half-round seams, you will have to add corresponding amounts of lead–tin solder in an extra step. If you solder for too long the iron will overheat and the lead–tin solder will get too soft and you will not be able to apply it properly. Turn the iron off for a while, before carrying on.

You can make a loop for hanging up a small mirror or glass picture out of copper wire and solder it to a seam. Use pliers to hold the copper wire in the desired position because it will get very hot during soldering.

A more robust way of hanging up larger mirrors and pictures will be necessary, and the weight of the whole object will have to be distributed over several soldered seams. For this purpose you will need thin steel strips (or cames), which can be bought in most craft shops. Stick further strips of copperfoil on to the back of the object over both vertical and horizontal soldering seams. Paint the foil with soldering fluid. Cut the steel strips to the required length and lay them across the newly laid copperfoil lines, soldering them together with lead–tin solder. There is no need to solder along the entire length of the steel strips, but you should apply solder at the edges of the object and at all crossing points. A loop of copper wire can be added to this grid of steel strips by soldering the loop to the steel strip at two points or by bending the ends of the steel strips into loops.

When you are applying the fine solder try to make delicate, half-round solder seams, even if you find it difficult to begin with.

A copper wire hanger should be sufficient for small objects.

Copper foil is stuck to the back of the mirror so that the laminate is not scratched. The ends of the steel strips can be bent into loops with pliers.

You have created your very first glass object.

Patinating

After soldering, you should clean your work thoroughly again, then, if you wish, the soldered seams can be patinated.

It is possible to patinate the silvery tin seams to give a more harmonious overall appearance, especially if you have used glass of warm colours. The tin seams tend to reflect light, and this can divert attention from the beautiful glass segments, which would look more effective if the seams had a matt finish.

You can buy copper-coloured or black patina, and it is applied with a small sponge or cloth. Wear rubber gloves because the patina contains acid that will affect your hands. Patinating is a kind of artificial oxidizing, a process that takes some time to achieve. The longer the patina is allowed to work, the more thoroughly the surface is oxidized, which means that there will be less risk of any parts becoming shiny again when the object is cleaned. Nevertheless, soon after patinating you should clean your object again, as the acid in the patina, if too concentrated and allowed to react for too long, will corrode the metal. I would suggest that you put the object in the bath-tub after patinating it and give it a lukewarm shower. You can dry the glass pieces with paper towel, but try to avoid touching the patinated seams.

If you are still not satisfied with the results of patinating — if the patina is not dark enough or individual shiny patches are visible, for example — you can repeat the process. Remember, too, that although the soldered seams may look very dark at first, they will lighten as they dry, which can take up to two weeks.

Copper-coloured patina will darken a little with age, and the mirror will acquire a timeless look.

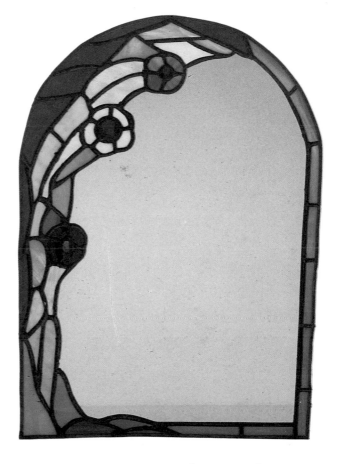

The dark, almost black patina on this mirror enhances the glass particularly well.

Many ideas can be realized in glass, even such frivolous things as this tree, clouds and bird.

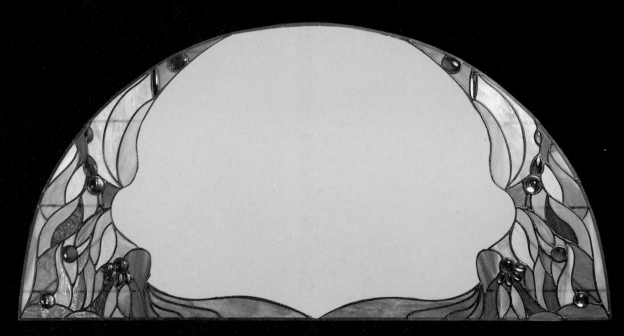

The frame of this semicircular dressing-table mirror is set with glass 'jewels' and 'diamonds'.

These mirrors are especially attractive as they have little 'balconies' for plants. However, if you put plants in them you must remember that glass, unlike clay, cannot breathe, so water can only evaporate with difficulty.

3. Projects

Project 1 — A Lampshade

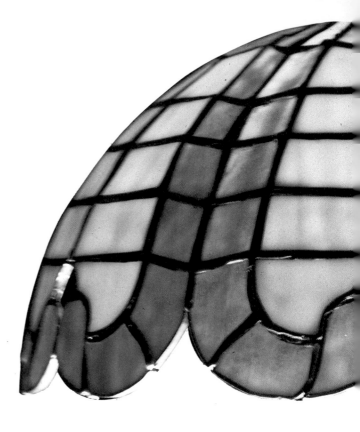

When you buy a kit for a lampshade a Styrofoam segment and cardboard templates are usually included.

The cardboard templates can be used immediately to draw on to the appropriate pieces of glass. As a rule, the Styrofoam segment will represent the equivalent of one-sixth of the overall shade, and it is used as a mould to ensure that all six parts of the lampshade have the correct curvature. Among the cardboard templates you will find two longish strips of identical size; these have to be fixed as a border along the sides of the Styrofoam segment. Use pins to hold them in position. Now you can assemble one-sixth of the shade on this segment using the cut pieces of glass. Start with the bottom edge,

A Styrofoam segment with the shape of the lampshade sketched on it.

Use pins to hold the various pieces of glass in position.

Depending on the shape of the pattern, you should build the pieces of glass upwards horizontally or vertically.

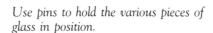

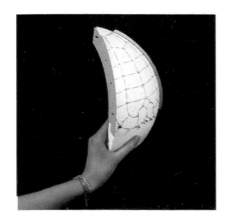

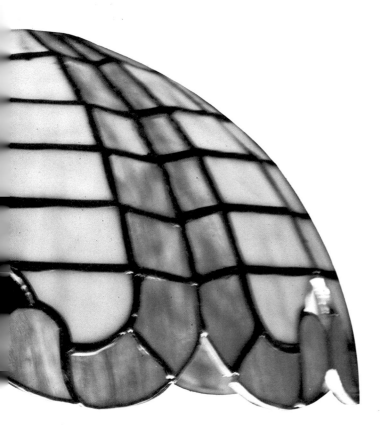

After that, the pieces of glass are spot soldered together in such a way that the segment is firm but still fairly pliable so that you will have enough 'play' when you are fitting the six segments together.

When you have made all six segments in this way, lay two segments at a time on to the Styrofoam segment and spot solder them; repeat this process with the other four pieces so that you have three 'thirds', which can be stood up on your workbench. You will now need an extra pair of hands to hold two of the 'thirds' together while you spot solder them. Finally, fit the third 'third'. Then you can start rough soldering, which must be done from the inside and then on the outside. Clean the lampshade thoroughly before proceeding to fine solder.

The caps you can buy are generally made of brass, and before you incorporate them into the shade, you should cover them with tin. Rub tallow over the cap and then apply a thin layer of tin using the soldering iron and lead–tin solder. When you come to fit the cap, make sure that it is positioned exactly in the centre of the lamp and not soldered in place crookedly. When everything is finished, the whole shade should be cleaned again before you can start patinating.

which should be fixed with pins in such a way that the edge is as straight as possible. Remember that the bottom edge of the shade will be most noticeable, so it should be worked very carefully. When you are satisfied with the bottom edge, build the lampshade segment upwards, working horizontally row by row or vertically in columns. Each piece of

glass is held in position with pins. Do not worry if a few pieces of glass protrude over the top edge. The cap, which will be inserted at the top of the lamp later on, will hide any uneven pieces.

When you have finished building up the first segment, the pieces have to be taken out, individually copperfoiled and then fitted together again.

After rough soldering, fit together two of the six segments on to the Styrofoam shape and spot solder them.

Fit the 'thirds' of the shade together on your workbench so that the bottom edge is straight.

Put a layer of tin over the cap before soldering it to the finished lampshade.

Plastic moulds

Some of the lampshade kits you can buy are assembled on fully shaped or hard plastic moulds. The lampshade can be completely assembled on one of these moulds before it is soldered. Do not fix the pieces with pins, however, but with double-sided adhesive tape of the kind you would, for example, use for carpet laying. When you have arranged all the pieces on the mould, you can still easily move a piece that was not cut correctly, alter it or replace it altogether. These moulds can be washed, so they can be used several times, and perhaps even used for your own design, which must be laid out and arranged on a three-dimensional mould if your lampshade is going to be curved. In some kits the pattern has already been drawn on the mould, but sometimes you may have to transfer a pattern to the mould yourself.

Lights

So far we have discussed curved or round lampshades — that is, lamps that cannot be made from a few flat pieces. Curved shades are much more common in Tiffany-style projects than free-standing, straight-sided lights, probably because Louis Comfort Tiffany, who was strongly influenced by Art Nouveau, is known to have used very few straight lines in his designs.

In the Art Deco period, however, an increasing number of lamps were designed to be assembled from several two-dimensional pieces, and obelisks and pyramids were especially popular at that time — for example, lamps were made of four equilateral triangles and a base plate. It is difficult to obtain ready-made patterns for this kind of light, but if you want to make a light in this style you should dispense with Styrofoam sheets when you assemble the various pieces. It is essential that the straight lines really are straight, and it is better to work on a board. For example, if you want to build a pyramid, you should lay the design of one of the four triangles on to a wooden board and nail two wooden battens along two sides of the triangle. In this way you can work on the four triangles one after the other and be sure they are exactly the same size. In addition, when you place the pieces of glass within the battens you will be able to see whether the edges are ground sufficiently. The individual pieces can be pinned to the pattern inside the battens. You should, therefore, use a board made of wood that is not so hard that the pins cannot penetrate it.

A hard plastic mould will allow you to design your own pattern for a lampshade. Either cut out a suitable piece of tracing-paper and stick it to the mould or draw straight on to the plastic.

You will need a board for working on segments with straight edges. The wooden battens are nailed along the outside edges of the shapes.

An Art Deco lamp made of equilateral triangles. The tops of the triangles were cut off so that the cap could be attached.

This dome-shaped lamp with a wavy lower edge gives out a lot of light.

A plain lampshade in warm colours will fit into almost any decor.

A shade mounted on a small caryatid made of bronze and based on an original Tiffany design.

This shade with a border of flowers could be used for a standing lamp or for a ceiling light.

39

This dragon-fly lamp is set with many glass 'jewels' and chased at the edges. Tin-plated copper filigree was soldered on to the wings of the dragon-flies to imitate as closely as possible the structure of the wings.

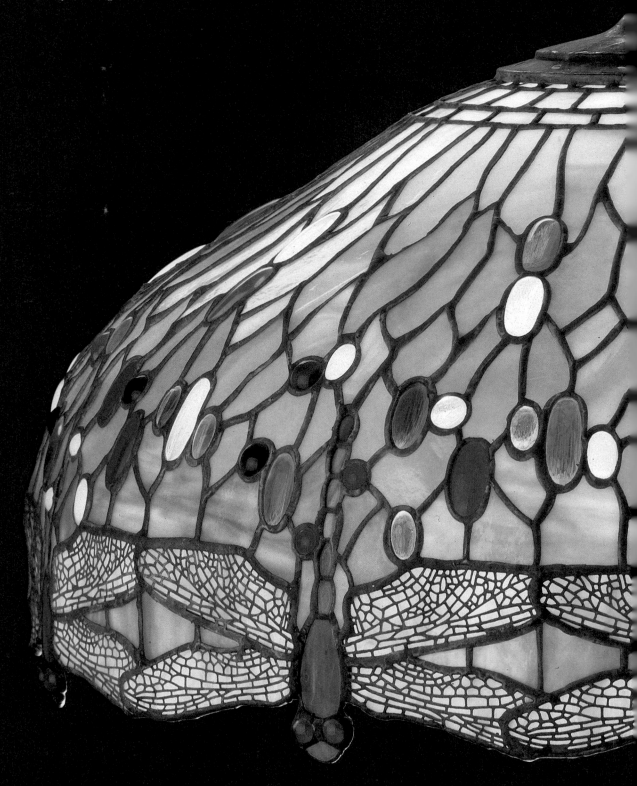

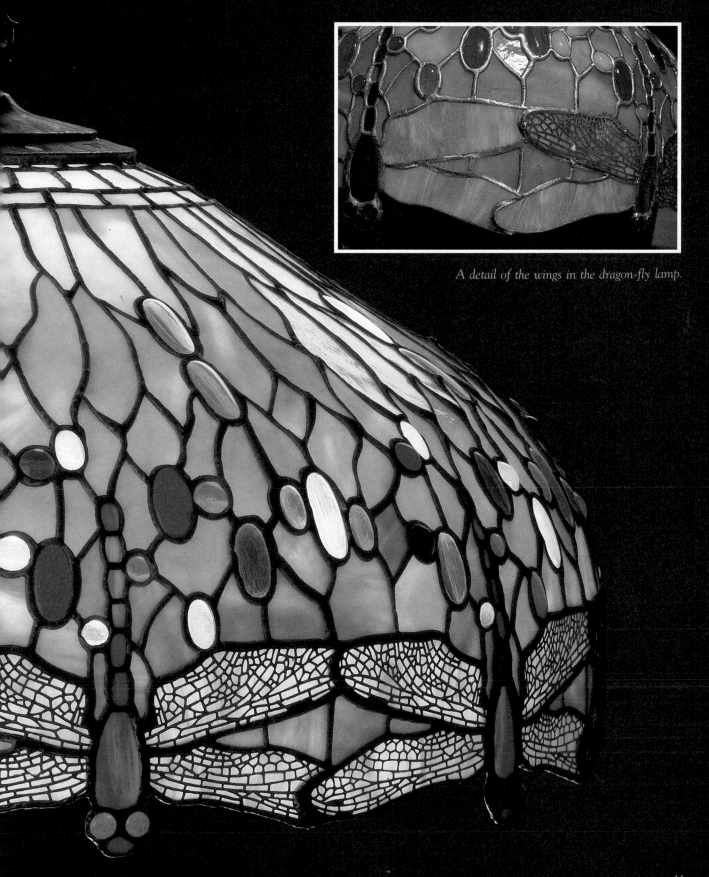

A detail of the wings in the dragon-fly lamp.

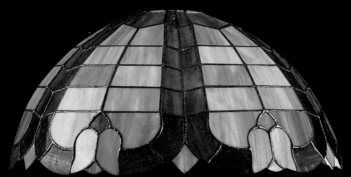

These Art Nouveau shades date from the turn of the century but are comparatively simple to make. They are especially suitable for table lamps. The different combinations of colours show how colour can change the character of an object, even if the shape remains the same.

Its size – the diameter is more than 50cm (19in) – and its subject – vine leaves and grapes – make this shade particularly suitable for illuminating a table.

Both sides of a shade with a peony motif, which derives its charm from the natural way the areas of red and green are distributed. Only a few extra tools were needed for the lead glazing.

Project 2 — Leading

It is not possible to describe the technique of leading in as great a detail as copperfoiling because of the limitations of space. Nevertheless, I will explain the process so that people using the Tiffany technique of copperfoiling will understand this other technique because both techniques can be combined easily with each other. If you are making large objects, especially those that are to be functional and will, therefore, be subject to considerable wear, you will have to use both techniques.

As leading is a completely separate technique, I have included a list of the tools that will be required.

Tools and materials

☆ Lead cames
☆ Lead knife
☆ A lathekin
☆ Lead nails (farrier's nails)
☆ Wire brush (not iron)
☆ Stearin oil or tallow
☆ A wood base to work on (this should be as large as the object being made)
☆ Wooden battens for edging the wood base

If you want to cut lead cames at an angle to form a mitre, which will always happen when you have to join two cames at a right angle, it is easy to squash the profile of the lead when you cut it. This can be avoided by inserting a knife or small piece of wood into the lead before you cut it and prising it back into shape.

Preparing to work

When you are leading always start with the frame. Fix the tracing-paper with the finished design to your wooden work base, then nail wooden battens along the outside lines of your design, starting with the base line and one of the two sides of the design. To make things simple, I have assumed that the object you are making is rectangular or square — a glass window, for example. The first two lead cames should be fitted along the angle formed by the two wooden battens.

Only a few additional tools and materials are needed for leading.

The lower part of the lead came that lies on the wooden base can be smoothed out with a lathekin.

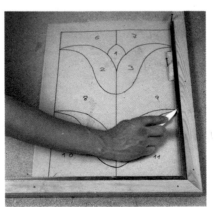

Stretching the lead

Lead is a comparatively soft material, which bends easily, and the cames, which generally have an H-shaped profile, are prone to being bent when they are transported or even when you are working, so they have to be straightened. Before you start leading, the cames must be stretched. To begin with, you may break a few pieces of lead by pulling them too hard, but you will soon gain the necessary experience and be able to judge how hard to pull each came. It is not possible to stretch all the pieces of lead you will be using before you begin. You should stretch only the one or two pieces that you will need immediately, and then stretch the next lengths as your work progresses.

Cutting the lead

After stretching the lead, score it lightly with a lead knife at the point you wish to cut it. Then, on each side of the mark, wedge two small pieces of wood into the H-shaped grooves of the lead came. This will prevent your freshly stretched came being deformed when you cut it with a knife. Use a slightly oscillating cutting movement to cut through the lead at the position you marked until you meet the little pieces of wood. Now you can remove them and cut through the remainder of the strip.

Assembly

Generally speaking, the leaded pieces are built up in a diagonal fashion from bottom to top. To ensure that the finished article is stable, it is extremely important that the pieces of glass are fixed in the sequence of their weight-bearing function. Work diagonally from a bottom corner to an opposite top corner so that you gain width and height at the same time. The angle of the wooden battens should prevent you from putting pieces in too loosely so that they later slip or from fixing them together too tightly.

First, place the ends of the stretched lead cames into the right angle formed by the battens and lay one over the other. Then score the top came to form a mitre — that is, in a line running from the corner at an angle of 45 degrees to the opposite corner. You are, in effect, marking a triangle that will be removed. Then swap the cames around and repeat the process. Then cut both cames to form a neat mitre, again using the little pieces of wood to keep the

Important: *when you are leading, you need not grind the edges of the glass, especially if you have cut them precisely.*

The first lead cames are fitted into the angle formed by the wooden battens.

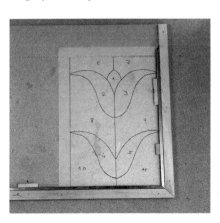

You can avoid squashing the strip when you cut it by inserting a piece of wood or glass into the profile.

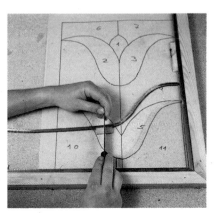

After cutting through the top part of the came, remove the little pieces of wood, and the remainder can be cut easily and without damaging the strip.

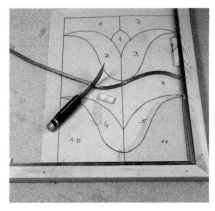

cames in shape. The two cames are then laid together at an angle and fixed into position. So that you do not damage the lead, nails are not driven immediately along the strip. First, you should insert a small piece of wood between the strip and the nail. As a rule, four nails — one at each end and one for each long side of the cames — should be sufficient. After fixing, the two cames should be soldered at the mitred join. (In order to proceed systematically I will describe the order of assembly before explaining the soldering process. This corner is the only spot that has to be soldered before the frame is finished.)

After soldering this one corner, lay the first piece of glass in the frame. Open the came slightly with a lathekin so that the piece of glass can be slid into the H-shape without damaging it. Use the handle of your lead knife to slide the glass into the came. Then stretch, prepare and cut the two cames needed to frame the

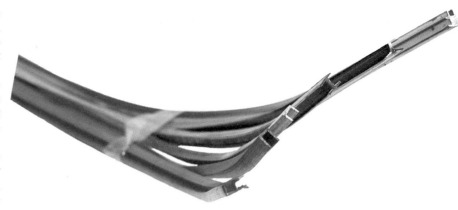

other sides of the piece of glass. One end of each of these two cames will, of course, meet the two frame cames. So that they can be slipped into the frame cames, the ends of these cames have to be pushed together with the handle of your knife. After squeezing together the end of the came in this way, slide it over the edge of the glass and then insert the end into the groove of the frame came.

Before leading the final open side of the first piece of glass, the first came around the piece of glass has to be fixed into position with lead nails and small pieces of wood. Before you do this, tap the piece of glass — again using the handle of your knife — in the direction of the soldered corner so that there is no play left in the grooves of the came. Then, when you have positioned and fixed the

You will need a little practice in cutting the lead cames to form mitres.

Before you slide the piece of glass into the side of the lead came, open out the came a little with a lathekin. Insert the lathekin at an angle and run it down the entire length of the came.

Use the handle of your knife to push the piece of glass into the groove in the came.

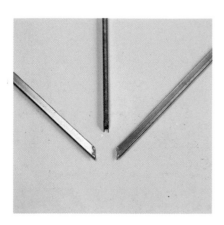

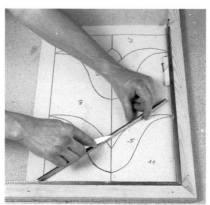

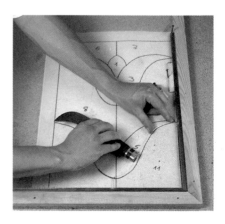

next lead came, you can begin to insert the next piece of glass.

Continue to build up the design in this way. When the whole area has been completely filled, it will be bordered on two sides by the angle of the wooden battens, while the other two sides can be held firmly in place with lead nails.

Framing

The end of the came protruding at the side of the bottom edge will have to be cut to an angle now to form a mitre. You should have left this until last because the whole design will have been slipping slightly while you were working, and the piece of glass bordering this corner will have to be removed temporarily.

Finally, all the lead cames with ends protruding over the edge of the open side will have to be cut in the right place. Score the strips with your knife so that the outer edges of the pieces of glass protrude beyond the cames by about 2mm (just over 1⁄16in) — that is, the lead cames should not quite reach the outer edges of the pieces of glass. Now take out the pieces of glass on this side, cut the cames and replace the glass. You do not need to fix this side again with lead nails. Push each piece of glass firmly into the grooves of the cames and carefully press the lead onto the glass. The lead came that you have prepared for the frame side should now be cut to fit the mitred corner and fitted to the edge of the object. Place the strip so that the edge of the glass fits into the groove and tap it so that the glass is pushed as deeply as possible into the groove. Now fix the frame came with lead nails.

Bend the top ends of the two side cames outwards so that you cut them at an angle to form the mitre. Do not take out the corner pieces of glass again because the design, which has now been completely fixed into position, could easily slip again. The top frame came is positioned and fixed last of all. To finish off, pass your lathekin over all the cames to make sure they are smooth.

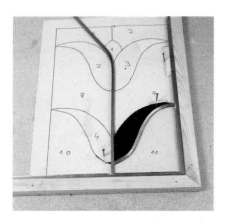

The pieces of glass and lead cames are fixed to the board with lead nails.

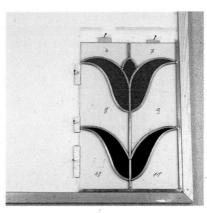

Before you set in the last two lead cames, solder all the other joints.

Press the lead cames down on to the glass with a lathekin.

Soldering

Lead and tin solder have almost the same melting points. You must, therefore, make sure that the temperature of the soldering iron remains even and is not too high. Check the temperature before you begin on a scrap of lead and a piece of soldering wire. The tin solder should melt but the lead should not.

Before you start soldering, all the points at which the lead cames meet should be cleaned carefully with a wire brush. Rub stearin oil or tallow (not soldering fluid) on to these joints, and then solder the joints with a drop of tin solder. When you come to solder the joints with the frame make sure that you do not solder beyond the centre of each came. This is because, when you have finished soldering, a steel strip will be laid around the bottom and side frame cames to give the whole object more stability and to make it possible to hang it up or fasten it securely. Push the steel band into the outside groove of the cames and fix it in position by bending over the edge

of the frame cames with your lathekin, first from the front, then from the back, so that the steel band can no longer be seen from the side and a smooth outer edge is created. Any solder joints that went over the centre of the frame strips would leave ugly lumps in the frame when you bend the came over the steel band, which is why you should be careful when soldering. After soldering, the stearin oil or tallow must be thoroughly cleaned off or a further chemical reaction will cause ugly stains to appear. When you have cleaned the front, turn the object over and solder the reverse side. Again, first smooth the strips with your lathekin.

If you have made a large picture or mirror using the copperfoiling technique, I would advise you to fix a lead came around the edge to make sure it is stable. The soldered seams should end about 5mm (¼in) from the edge. Then you can lay a lead came around the edge of the object and solder it with copperfoil, which will also finish off the soldered seams. Use tallow as a flux.

Before positioning the two last lead cames, the two cames already fixed to these sides have to be cut off about 2mm (just over ¹⁄₁₆in) from the edge of the glass so that the frame cames can overlap the pieces of glass.

The solder points should be slightly roughened with a wire brush.

Lead cames are spot soldered at the joints.

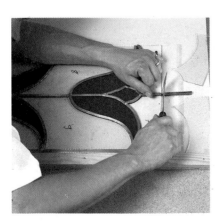

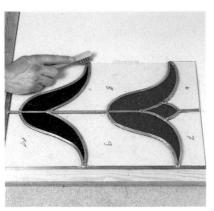

Lead glazing: a colourful semicircle made of antique glass and set in lead cames.

A steel band is laid into the H-profile of the frame cames.

Bend the lead came frame downwards with a lathekin.

To provide a secure means of hanging up the object, the ends of the steel band can be bent into loops with pliers.

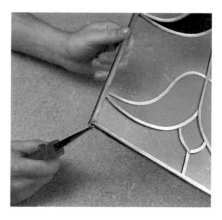

49

This window is a beautiful example of the brilliance of coloured antique glass.

The impact of these straight lines is emphasized by the use of only two colours.

Two examples of typical Victorian-style lead glazing

Rural charm is the keynote in this picture with its agricultural motif, which would suit a country-style interior.

Project 3 — A Terrarium

When you make a terrarium or planter it is absolutely essential that you are adept at creating long, straight cuts. Draw two dots on a piece of glass and lay your rubber-backed metal ruler against them. Pass the flat side of the glass cutter along the ruler, remembering that even on this side of the cutter a gap of about 2mm (1/16in) will be created. This fractional amount will have to be taken into account when you draw

When you are making long cuts along a ruler, make sure that the glass cutter does not cause the ruler to slip.

To make the terrarium shown above you will need the following pieces of glass:
Roof
One piece of window glass 39.5 × 9cm (15½ × 3½in)
One piece of window glass 39.5 × 13.5cm (15½ × 5½in)
Two triangles of window glass 9 × 13.5 × 15.5cm (3½ × 5½ × 6in)
Long sides
Two pieces of window glass 39.5 × 14.5cm (15½ × 5¾in)
Two pieces of opalescent glass 39.5 × 5cm (15½ × 2in)
Short sides
Two pieces of window glass 15.5 × 14.5cm (6 × 5¾in)
Two pieces of opalescent glass 15.5 × 5cm (6 × 2in)
Base (optional)
One piece of window glass 39.5 × 15.5cm (15½ × 6in)

Move the cutter towards you when you make long cuts.

First, solder the pieces of one side.

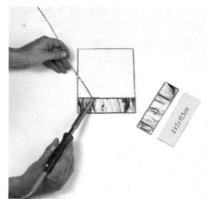

In order to solder a short side of the terrarium at an angle of 90 degrees to the long side, the long side has to be supported against a heavy object.

the line, otherwise your piece of glass will turn out too small. Draw the glass cutter towards your body, as this helps to create an even movement over long stretches. You should also make sure that you cut along the inside of the line you have drawn, as grinding large plates of glass later on is a very tedious job. The more closely your cut follows the line you have drawn, the less work you will have when you come to grind the edge, which can, in itself, create irregularities. I would recommend that you make a few practice cuts using ordinary window glass and cut a few narrow strips off the edge of a large sheet of glass before you begin to cut the glass for your project.

Before you begin the foiling process, you should think about whether to use tinned (silver-coloured) copperfoil. This is usually recommended for terraria for visual reasons.

First, prepare and finish one of the long, narrow sides of the terrarium, and spot solder it. The short side can then be fitted to it vertically, but before you do this you will have to anchor the long side in the required position. Stand it against a heavy object or wedge it into position in such a way that it is standing upright on your work table. When you have

attached all the four sides to each other and spot soldered them, you can finish soldering the first part of the terrarium. Make sure you hold the seams horizontally, not vertically, as you solder them, otherwise too much tin would run downwards.

When you build the roof you are going to need a helper who can hold the roof sections at the correct angles. You might find it useful to cut out a little cardboard template and fix it to the join with adhesive tape. Spot solder the roof until it sits firmly. Now check the side triangles, again using a cardboard template, as it is impossible to avoid irregularities when you are making an object of this size. Now cut out the glass triangles, using your template, to fit the empty spaces in the roof section, position them and solder then in place. Now the terrarium is ready and is stable enough to be soldered properly.

You can either use a plastic seed tray (as illustrated) or, if you do not like this idea, a piece of glass for the base of the terrarium. This can be measured precisely and fitted right at the end. If you decide to fit a glass floor, make sure that the terrarium is sealed by coating the bottom edges of the terrarium with a transparent rubber solution before planting.

Using Off-cuts

One of the most pleasing aspects of making things out of glass is that you can even use the leftovers.

Generally, of course, you will only be able to use up your off-cuts properly after you have completed several Tiffany-style objects because only then will you have accumulated enough small pieces of glass in different shapes and colours. So, do not throw anything away but collect all your leftover pieces in a box.

With the experience you have gained in making a mirror or lampshade, the making of small objects should hardly present any problems at all. A little present that is suddenly needed or a small thank-you gift can be quickly made with little trouble and at hardly any cost. A few ideas for small presents, accessories and ornaments are shown on the pages that follow, but there should be no limit to your inventiveness, and in time you will be able to add other attractive little objects to these examples.

When you are finishing the soldering, hold the terrarium in such a way that the seams run horizontally, so that the tin solder does not drip downwards.

Note: *you will need a helper when you come to solder the roof.*

Always try to solder the corresponding inner and outer edges in one operation.

If you prefer, use a plastic seed tray as a base.

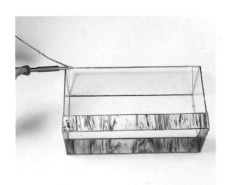

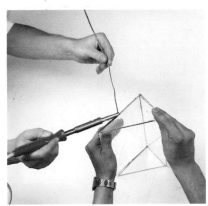

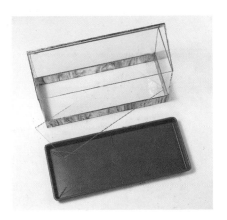

Glass off-cuts need not end up in the dustbin. These attractive little animals and insects are especially popular with children, while fragments of mirror combined with a few bits of coloured glass can be turned into decorative pocket mirrors, which would find a home in any handbag.

There need be no limits to your inventiveness when using up leftover pieces of glass.

Glass is very versatile. Here, a tabletop has been made of iridescent Merry-go-round glass, and on it stands a jewellery box made of the tiniest pieces of glass.

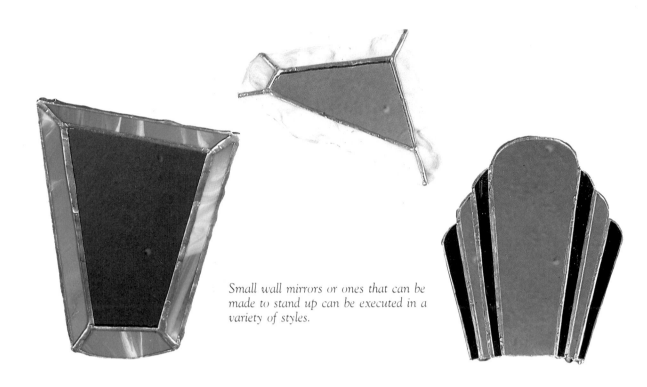

Small wall mirrors or ones that can be
made to stand up can be executed in a
variety of styles.

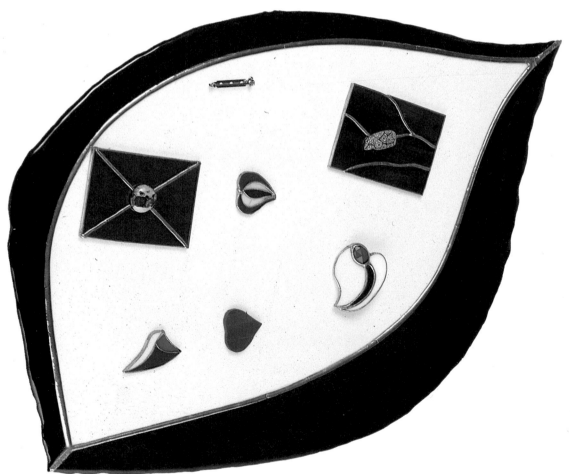

The tiniest shards can be turned into brooches, earrings or pendants.

Small glass images with Christmas motifs make festive window ornaments.

4. Ideas for Glass Projects

Even quite large plants will fit into this terrarium as the roof can be removed.

This small house was quickly made and the colour of the glass could be altered to suit different kinds of flowers.

Delicate, exotic plants will thrive in this unusual but dainty terrarium.

The mirrored back of this hanging terrarium makes these colourful plants appear even more prolific.

This dainty planter makes an attractive setting for small foliage plants.

61

This Chinese pagoda planted with creepers would be a decorative feature in any room.

The rich colours of the flowers go extremely well with this colourful terrarium. A scale drawing of the side panels is given on page 79.

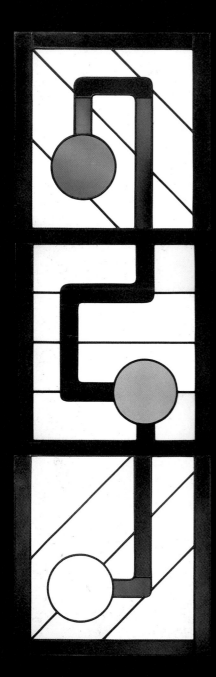

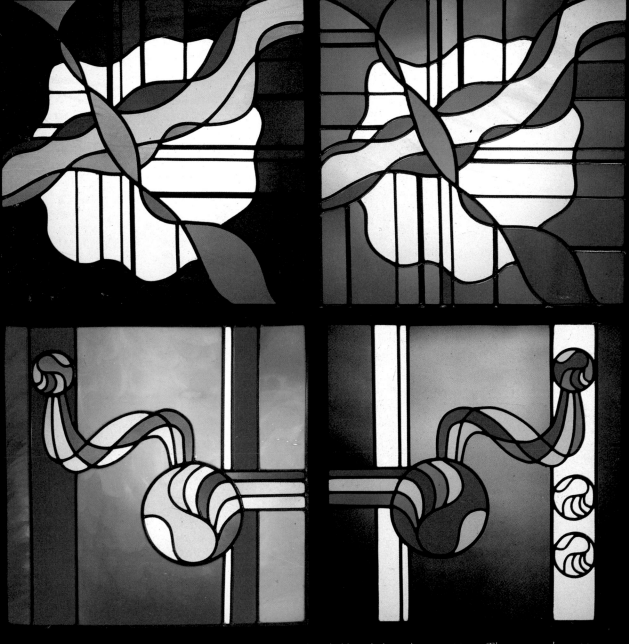

Abstract shapes combine with complementary colours to produce bold yet balanced compositions. The very modern appearance of these pictures vividly demonstrates the timeless quality of glass as a medium.

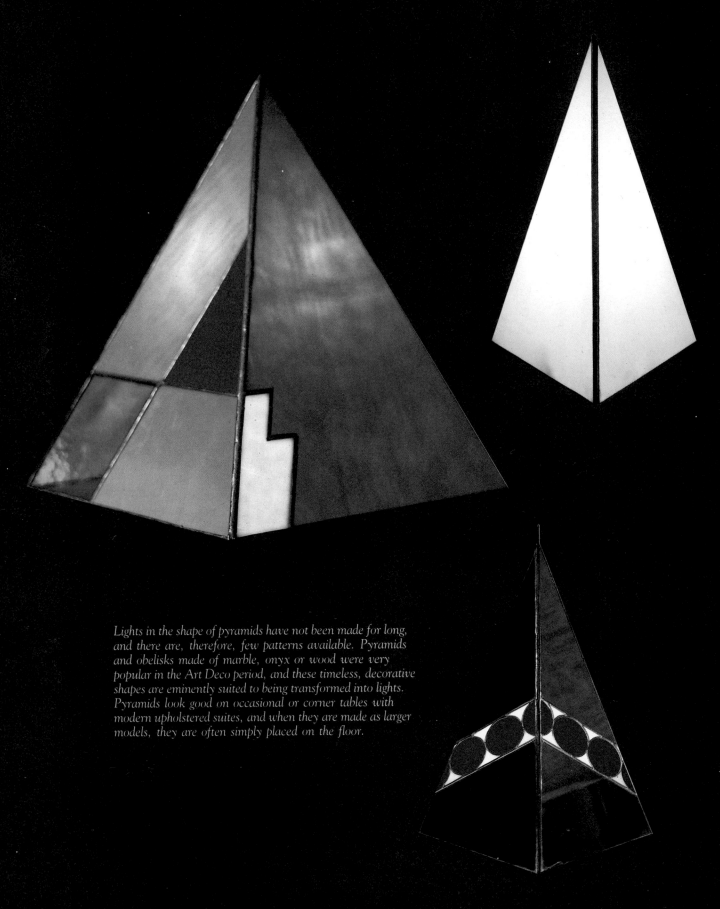

Lights in the shape of pyramids have not been made for long, and there are, therefore, few patterns available. Pyramids and obelisks made of marble, onyx or wood were very popular in the Art Deco period, and these timeless, decorative shapes are eminently suited to being transformed into lights. Pyramids look good on occasional or corner tables with modern upholstered suites, and when they are made as larger models, they are often simply placed on the floor.

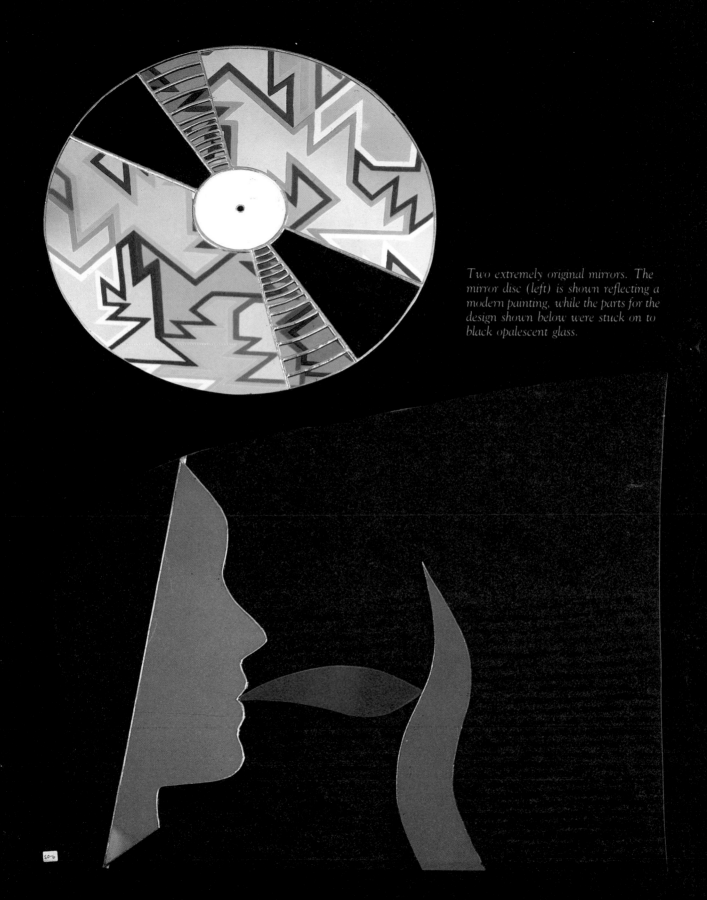

Two extremely original mirrors. The mirror disc (left) is shown reflecting a modern painting, while the parts for the design shown below were stuck on to black opalescent glass.

A fantastic landscape executed in splendid, richly coloured opalescent glass. The structure of the multicoloured antique glass captures the colours of the sky especially well.

This Art Nouveau piece, with its graceful plant ornaments, is particularly suitable for large windows in high rooms.

Interesting results can be achieved by constantly repeating simple shapes. Very 'busy' compositions can be successfully executed in a single colour as glass can be found with the most delicate range of tonal gradations.

These wall pictures could be used to create accents in a very individually decorated room.

A bamboo lampshade based on an original Tiffany design.

This so-called Baroque lampshade is one of the most popular of all Art Nouveau motifs.

A table lamp with a shade made out of eight segments of only two kinds of glass.

This pendent lamp in the Art Deco style demands surroundings to match.

A ceiling lightshade made in the same style as the table lamp on the previous page but in different colours.

This small lamp creates a warm, comfortable atmosphere.

This shade, which is decorated with a small flower, spreads a gentle, pastel-coloured light.

This pillar of light is made of mirrors. It is closed at the top, but a half-open glass lozenge-shape makes it suitable as a pedestal for vases or plants.

A mirror with a flowing edge of opalescent glass.

An unusual clock with an inlaid dial of gold mirror glass and contrasting black opalescent glass surround.

This light stele or pillar allows light to pass from the inside through the glass motifs. Ornaments with a lot of detail are not as successful in large light pillars, which are more effective when viewed from a distance. Pop-art motifs can be used to advantage in this kind of light.

75

5. Using Grids and Scale Drawings

Grids

When you make glass pictures and windows and mirrors you have to reproduce the design you have created yourself or have adapted from another source to fit the size of the planned object. To do this you should use a grid. For example, if you want to use the design for an apple-shaped mirror shown opposite in a different size, you should first measure exactly the length and width of the design. The proportions of the length and width cannot be varied, and the proportions of the finished design will be the same whether the design is enlarged or reduced.

To enlarge a design proportionately, lay it on a large piece of tracing-paper and draw a diagonal line from the bottom left-hand corner, through the top right-hand corner and right across the tracing-paper. At any point along this diagonal line you can draw a perpendicular line to the base line; the point at which the perpendicular line bisects the base will give the desired width. If you then draw a horizontal line from the point at which the diagonal and vertical lines cross to the left edge, you will automatically obtain a proportionately enlarged area.

Once you have determined the new size, draw the outline of the original design — that is, the square or rectangle of measured sides — on tracing-paper and divide it up into a grid of equal-sized squares. Then lay the tracing-paper over the design so that you can trace the lines of the design on to the paper.

Just as you enlarged the original, you must now enlarge the individual grid squares. Work out the new grid size by using a multiple of the measurements of the original grid. If, for example, the grid squares on the small piece of tracing-paper are 2 × 2cm (approximately 1 × 1in), then you could multiply this by three to give a proportionately larger grid; in this instance, each square would be 6 × 6cm (approximately 3 × 3in). The multiple you select must, of course, fill the large area you have already drawn.

Because you are enlarging proportionately, you will not have any difficulty in finding a multiplier (or, in the case of a reductions, a divisor) to determine the size of the grid squares. Now draw these grid squares on the new area — that is, on the tracing-paper on which you marked the diagonal to determine the new size.

You do not have to be an accomplished artist to transfer the outlines of the apple that show through in the grid squares of the original design to the corresponding grid squares of the larger design. If you are working on a complicated design, it is a good idea to number the grid squares.

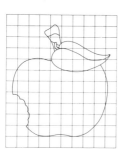

A grid drawn on tracing-paper can be used to enlarge a small design.

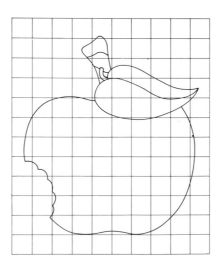

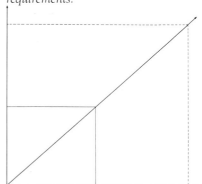

Draw a diagonal to help you vary the size of the design to suit your requirements.

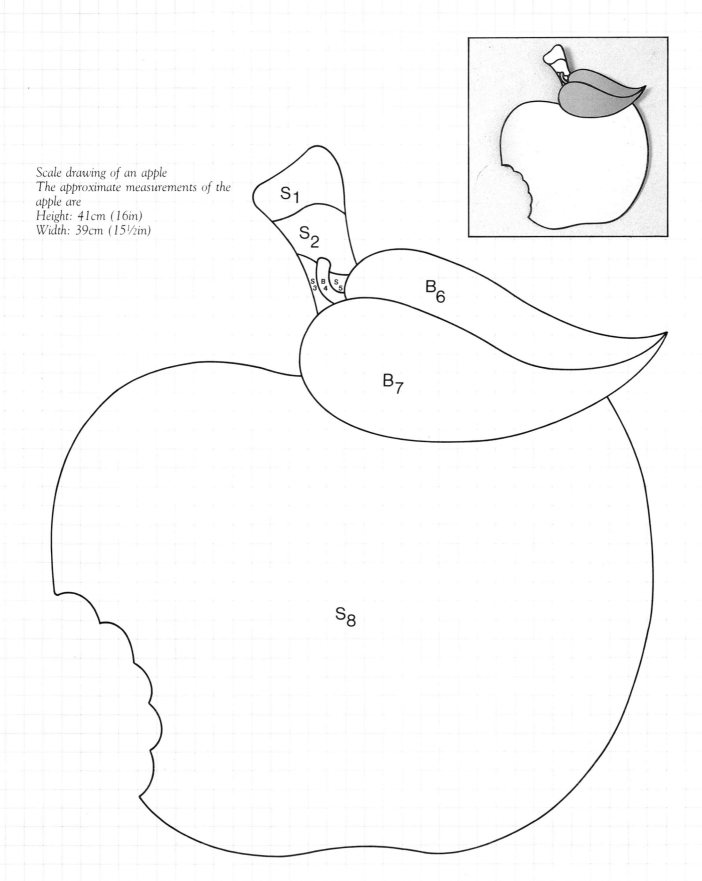

Scale drawing of an apple
The approximate measurements of the
apple are
Height: 41cm (16in)
Width: 39cm (15½in)

S₁

S₂

S₃ B₄ S₅

B₆

B₇

S₈

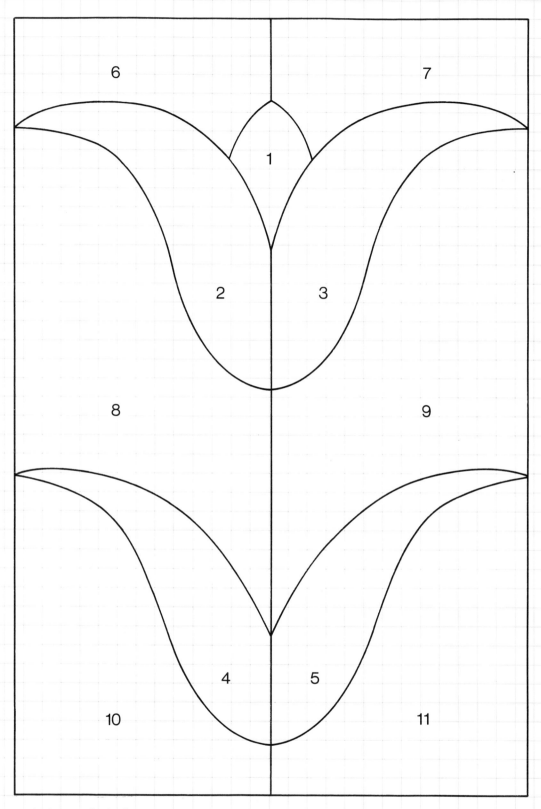

Scale diagram for leading project:
The object measures:
Height: 48cm (approximately 19in)
Width: 32cm (approximately 12½in)
(The finished leading of this motif is illustrated on page 48.)

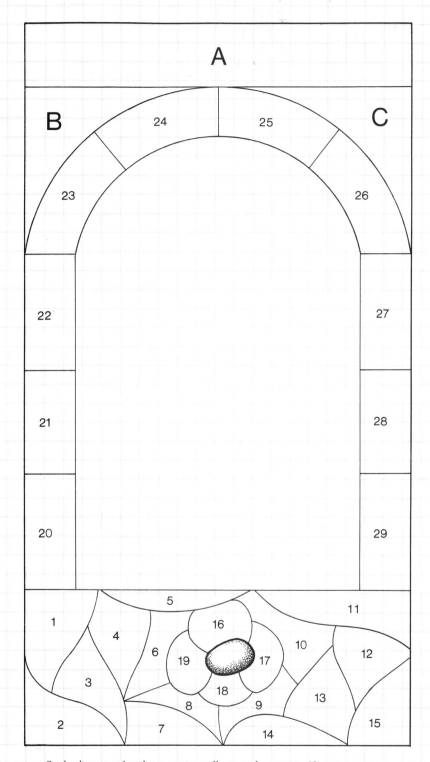

Scale diagram for the terrarium illustrated on page 63.
Overall size of panel: 28 × 15cm (11 × 6in)
Roof: six triangles of antique glass 15 × 20 × 20cm (6 × 8 × 8in)
Floor: one hexagon of window glass, each side 15cm (6in) long

Appendices

Metric Conversions

1 inch = 2.54cm
1 square inch = 6.45 square centimetres
1 foot = 0.304m
1 square foot = 929 square centimetres
1 pound = 0.4536kg

Copperfoil Widths

⅛ in = 3mm
³⁄₁₆in = 4.5mm
⁷⁄₃₂in = 5.5mm
¼in = 6.5mm
⁵⁄₁₆ = 8mm
⅜in = 10mm

Bibliography

On the life and work of Louis Comfort Tiffany:

Louis Comfort Tiffany (2 volumes), Hugh F. McKean, 1981

On glass windows:

The Art Glass Windows, John Forbes, Hidden House Publications, Phoenix/Arabeth, 1981

On ornaments:

Treasury of Traditional Stained Glass Designs, Ann V. Winterbotham, Dover Publications, New York, 1981

On small objects:

Stained Glass Gifts, Judy Miller, Hidden House Publications, Palo Alto, 1982

A BLANDFORD BOOK

First published in the UK 1991
by Blandford (a Cassell imprint)
Villiers House, 41/47 Strand, London WC2N 5JE
Reprinted 1992, 1994 (Twice)

Copyright © 1985 Falken Verlag GmbH, Niedernhausen/Ts., Germany
English translation © Astrid Mick 1991

Distributed in the United States
by Sterling Publishing Co., Inc.
387 Park Avenue South, New York, NY 10016–8810

Distributed in Australia
by Capricorn Link (Australia) Pty Ltd
P.O. Box 665, Lane Cove, NSW 2066

British Library Cataloguing in Publication Data
Koppel, Nikolaus
 Stained glass projects.
 1. Handicrafts using stained glass. Techniques
 I. Title II. Glaskunst in Tiffany — Technik, *English*
 748.5028
 ISBN 0–7137–2230–4

Printed in Singapore